"As For Me and My House"

Rev. Daniel L. Patrick

Edited By: T.L. Gray

Vabella Publishing

Vabella Publishing
P.O. Box 1052
Carrollton, Georgia 30112

©Copyright 2011 by Daniel L. Patrick

All rights reserved. No part of the book may be reproduced or utilized in any form or by any means without permission in writing from the author. All requests should be addressed to the publisher.

Manufactured in the United States of America

13-digit ISBN 978-1-938230-97-4

Library of Congress Cataloging-in-Publication Data

Patrick, Daniel L., 1952-
 As for me and my house / Daniel L. Patrick ; edited by Tonya Gray. -- 1st ed.
   p. cm.
 Includes bibliographical references and index.
 ISBN 978-0-9834332-1-7 (pbk. : alk. paper)
 1. Families--Biblical teaching. 2. Families--Religious life. I. Gray, Tonya
(Tonya L.), 1971- II. Title.
  BS680.F3P38 2011
  220.8'30685--dc22
                              2011016389

Acknowledgements

I want to sincerely thank my lovely wife Carla, who for over 40 years has loved me more than I deserve. This book is dedicated to her, my sons Joseph and Todd, my daughter-in-laws Mechelle and Deanna, and my grandchildren Elise, Bailey, Garrett and Luke. I thank them for their love, prayers and support. I also want to thank Pastors Kenneth & Jeanelle Dunn for their prayers and guidance over all the years.

Also special thanks to writer and author T.L. Gray for her devotion and dedication in making this book a reality. I thank all my minister friends God has sent my way. Most of all, the glory belongs to God who loves us so much He gave His only begotten Son!

Contents

Introduction 1

What is it to Serve God? 6

The Difference Between Men & Women 20

The Spiritual Responsibilities of Man 30

The Spiritual Responsibilities of Woman 37

The Sanctity of Marriage 45

The Responsibilities of Husband & Wife 54

Parental Duty 62

Finances 71

Communication 78

Intimacy 84

About the Author 90

Introduction

Joshua 24:1-25

¹And Joshua gathered all the tribes of Israel to Shechem, and called for the elders of Israel, and for their heads, and for their judges, and for their officers; and they presented themselves before God.

²And Joshua said unto all the people, Thus saith the LORD God of Israel, Your fathers dwelt on the other side of the flood in old time, even Terah, the father of Abraham, and the father of Nachor: and they served other gods.

³And I took your father Abraham from the other side of the flood, and led him throughout all the land of Canaan, and multiplied his seed, and gave him Isaac.

⁴And I gave unto Isaac Jacob and Esau: and I gave unto Esau mount Seir, to possess it; but Jacob and his children went down into Egypt.

⁵I sent Moses also and Aaron, and I plagued Egypt, according to that which I did among them: and afterward I brought you out.

⁶And I brought your fathers out of Egypt: and ye came unto the sea; and the Egyptians pursued after your fathers with chariots and horsemen unto the Red sea.

⁷And when they cried unto the LORD, he put darkness between you and the Egyptians, and brought the sea upon them, and covered them; and your eyes have seen what I have done in Egypt: and ye dwelt in the wilderness a long season.

⁸And I brought you into the land of the Amorites, which dwelt on the other side Jordan; and they fought with you: and I gave them into your hand, that ye might possess their land; and I destroyed them from before you.

⁹Then Balak the son of Zippor, king of Moab, arose and warred against Israel, and sent and called Balaam the son of Beor to curse you:

¹⁰But I would not hearken unto Balaam; therefore he blessed you still: so I delivered you out of his hand.

¹¹And you went over Jordan, and came unto Jericho: and the men of Jericho fought against you, the Amorites,

and the Perizzites, and the Canaanites, and the Hittites, and the Girgashites, the Hivites, and the Jebusites; and I delivered them into your hand.

^{12}And I sent the hornet before you, which drave them out from before you, even the two kings of the Amorites; but not with thy sword, nor with thy bow.

^{13}And I have given you a land for which ye did not labour, and cities which ye built not, and ye dwell in them; of the vineyards and oliveyards which ye planted not do ye eat.

^{14}Now therefore fear the LORD, and serve him in sincerity and in truth: and put away the gods which your fathers served on the other side of the flood, and in Egypt; and serve ye the LORD.

^{15}And if it seem evil unto you to serve the LORD, choose you this day whom ye will serve; whether the gods which your fathers served that were on the other side of the flood, or the gods of the Amorites, in whose land ye dwell: but as for me and my house, we will serve the LORD.

[16] And the people answered and said, God forbid that we should forsake the LORD, to serve other gods;

[17] For the LORD our God, he it is that brought us up and our fathers out of the land of Egypt, from the house of bondage, and which did those great signs in our sight, and preserved us in all the way wherein we went, and among all the people through whom we passed:

[18] And the LORD drave out from before us all the people, even the Amorites which dwelt in the land: therefore will we also serve the LORD; for he is our God.

[19] And Joshua said unto the people, Ye cannot serve the LORD: for he is an holy God; he is a jealous God; he will not forgive your transgressions nor your sins.

[20] If ye forsake the LORD, and serve strange gods, then he will turn and do you hurt, and consume you, after that he hath done you good.

[21] And the people said unto Joshua, Nay; but we will serve the LORD.

^{22}And Joshua said unto the people, Ye are witnesses against yourselves that ye have chosen you the LORD, to serve him. And they said, We are witnesses.

^{23}Now therefore put away, said he, the strange gods which are among you, <u>and incline your heart unto the LORD God of Israel</u>.

^{24}And the people said unto Joshua, The LORD our God will we serve, and his voice will we obey.

^{25}So Joshua made a covenant with the people that day, and set them a statute and an ordinance in Shechem.

Chapter 1

What is it to Serve God?

We often think to ourselves that we know what it means to serve God, but do we really? Do we truly understand what encompasses our duty and faithfulness to God?

Let me begin by taking us back to the beginning of Joshua 24 and point out a few things. First of all… Joshua gathered ALL the people of Israel[1], not just a select few, but everyone from the elders, judges and officials who had influence over the people, down to the common laborers and children. No one was exempt. No one was left out. Everyone was included regardless of social standing or moral condition. After Joshua gathered everyone, he presented them ALL to God, and then God began to speak to them through Joshua reminding them of His deliverance, protection and provision.

---

[1] *Joshua 24:1* - [1]*And Joshua gathered all the tribes of Israel to Shechem, and called for the elders of Israel, and for their heads, and for their judges, and for their officers; and they presented themselves before God. (KJV)*

Look at verses 14 & 15.² God reminded the people not to forget about what happened before the flood, and in contrast what was happening in the present day with their idol worship. In this particular passage, the word *evil* in the Hebrew means good for nothing, bad; physically, socially and morally wrong; wicked. The word *serve* in the Hebrew means to enslave, to keep in bondage, be a bondman or a bond servant.

Being in service to God does not put us in bondage as described above, but is a willing service. The difference between a slave and a bond servant is that a slave has no choice and receives no payment for his service, whereas a bond servant is free and serves by choice and receives some sort of payment or reward for fulfilling his duty. One is operated out of a physical demand, the other from a willing heart.

---

² *Joshua 24:14-15* -¹⁴*Now therefore fear the LORD, and serve him in sincerity and in truth: and put away the gods which your fathers served on the other side of the flood, and in Egypt; and serve ye the LORD.* ¹⁵*And if it seem evil unto you to serve the LORD, choose you this day whom ye will serve; whether the gods which your fathers served that were on the other side of the flood, or the gods of the Amorites, in whose land ye dwell: but as for me and my house, we will serve the LORD. (KJV)*

The simplicity of serving God comes down to a choice. The perplexity of it is to enslave ourselves to God, to die to self and our desires in order to fulfill His desires. If that isn't hard, I don't know what is. As my wife, Pastor Carla, once asked, "Who wants more of God?" Everyone raised their hands. She then answered, "Okay, if that's what you really want, then here's how you do it… Get rid of self."

This message was Joshua's last to the people of Israel before he died, so the importance of it is magnified. It's an ecclesiastical summation with as much relevance as, *"Let us hear the conclusion of the whole matter"*[3]. God impressed this message upon Joshua's heart and he declared, "As for me and my house, we will serve the Lord[4]." The children of Israel now had the same choice sitting before them. They could continue to serve their idols and live in darkness, or else put away those idols, remembering what God had

---

[3] Ecclesiastes 12:13 - [13]*Let us hear the conclusion of the whole matter: Fear God, and keep his commandments: for this is the whole duty of man. (KJV)*

[4] Joshua 24:15 - [15]*And if it seem evil unto you to serve the LORD, choose you this day whom ye will serve; whether the gods which your fathers served that were on the other side of the flood, or the gods of the Amorites, in whose land ye dwell: but as for me and my house, we will serve the LORD. (KJV)*

done for them and choose to serve Him only. It was a choice of commitment, truth and sincerity.

The Power of Such a Decision

[5]This is a decision of total commitment, unconditional surrender where we are to be loyal and faithful to God. We are not to serve God based on what we want to do, but on what He asks us to do. It involves turning away from the world and all of its philosophies, and taking a stand for the teachings of Christ.

In [6]Romans 12:1 & 2 the word *beseech* means to strongly adhere. We are to bring or offer ourselves as a living sacrifice unto God. He's not to carry us, we are to carry ourselves. *Conform* means to be transformed or transfigured. We've been delivered from the power of darkness. I want you to understand that darkness has

---

[5] <u>Joshua 24:20</u> - [20]*If ye forsake the LORD, and serve strange gods, then he will turn and do you hurt, and consume you, after that he hath done you good. (KJV)*

[6] <u>Romans 12:1-2</u> - [6]*I beseech you therefore, brethren, by the mercies of God, that ye present your bodies a living sacrifice, holy, acceptable unto God, which is your reasonable service.* [2]*And be not conformed to this world: but be ye transformed by the renewing of your mind, that ye may prove what is that good, and acceptable, and perfect, will of God. (KJV)*

power. If we're not careful, we can be transformed or transfigured to this world. But we've been delivered, from the power of darkness and this *world* – the age or time in which we live.

Today, right now... this truth is pertinent and just as powerful as the day it was penned. However, we shouldn't try to bring God into the twenty-first century. That's what we try to do. We should take the twenty-first century to God. What I mean by that is... we often say and think, "Oh, God... hey, it's the twenty-first century and people do things different than they used to. I know back then people had different ideas, different habits, and lived in a different culture; it's really not relevant to us today." Oh, but Saints of God, it is! God knew back when He penned this passage in the time of Romans what would happen in the twenty-first century. God never changes[7]. He is the same yesterday, today and forever[8]. Conforming God to this world is trying to get God to change according to the time and social acceptance in which we live. We have got to start

---

[7] *Malachi 3:6* - *⁶For I am the LORD, I change not; therefore ye sons of Jacob are not consumed. (KJV)*

[8] *Hebrews 13:8* - *⁸Jesus Christ the same yesterday, and today, and forever. (KJV)*

thinking differently! God doesn't change in holiness, righteousness or mercy. We can't think that God's approval is on everything we do.

A religious change in our life doesn't constitute a transformation. There's a world of difference between transformation and change. A change is on the outside, but a transformation happens in the heart of a man and change follows. We must choose to follow God and not man; and it must be done with a willing heart and mind. Christian homes MUST be willing to go against the flow of society; to resist what everybody else is doing. God's word is true and precise and goes against our fleshly desires. God is not politically correct. He's not going to please everybody and every style of living. He's not trying to win votes or be at the top of some poll. The power of the decision to be a household that serves God is one of life and death.

In [9]Deuteronomy 30:19 Moses spoke with the same intensity as Joshua had earlier, emphasizing the importance of what he had to say. Here again, the people

---

[9] *Deuteronomy 30:19* - *[19]I call heaven and earth to record this day against you, that I have set before you life and death, blessing and cursing: therefore choose life, that both thou and thy seed may live: (KJV)*

of Israel are given a choice to choose life or death, blessings or cursing. But, look at why they were given a choice… so that they and their seed would live.

Every day we choose whether to go, or not go; do or not do; speak or remain silent, be ill-tempered or at peace, and so forth. It's our choice regardless of the circumstances.

In [10]I Kings 18:21 the question Elijah proposes to the people infers that they were flirting between two decisions, to serve God or not to serve Him. That sounds a lot like today's church. Most of us serve God according to what we **think** God would have us do instead of reading about it in the Word of God. We're flirting between two decisions saying things like, "I can be a Christian and still do this." Or "I can be a Christian and still say this."

Elijah said, *"If the Lord be God, follow Him."* Just as Joshua provoked the people of Israel, in a sense challenging them to make a decision, Elijah does the same here. They both knew that there needed to be a

---

[10] <u>1 Kings 18:21</u> - *²¹And Elijah came unto all the people, and said, How long halt ye between two opinions? if the LORD be God, follow him: but if Baal, then follow him. And the people answered him not a word. (KJV)*

change in the people's lives because of participation in some activities contrary to God's laws. Don't be caught between two decisions. Make a choice. We can't be wishy-washy about it. If we determine God is God, then we must serve Him in obedience.

The Problems of Such a Decision

The word *hate* in the Greek means to detest; to persecute; to be hateful toward. If we or our families are looking for popularity, then Christianity isn't going to work for us. How do I know? That's what Jesus said in [11]John 15:18. He said the world is going to hate us, because it hated Him first.

What I mean by Christianity is someone who is a follower of Christ and His teachings. Religious philosophy or actions mixed with the world's ways does not make Christianity. Just like Elijah and Joshua proclaimed earlier, this statement is plain and to the point and will not be popular. It's not popular to be a Christian family in the world today. It never was and

---

[11] *John 15:18* - [18]*If the world hate you, ye know that it hated me before it hated you.* (KJV)

never will be. If we (the Christian) were of the world, it would love us back, but it doesn't.[12]

The word *world* in the Greek means its inhabitants and morality. There's a great deal of pressure put on Christian families to be loved by the world. Yet Jesus said that because we've been chosen out of the world, it will hate us. Remember what the word hate means? According to this scripture, we will be persecuted, detested and hated. We will be unpopular. If we don't want that sort of treatment in our life, more than likely we'll compromise our beliefs. We all want a religious belief that will be loved by the world and the church, but that's not possible.

We live in a day and age where we Christians want to keep our beliefs to ourselves. When we go among the world, we don't even let them know we go to church, keeping quiet and laughing at their jokes. That's wrong. We do this to keep from being offended or to keep from offending someone else, or to fit in. We need to understand the implications of what Joshua said, and

---

[12] <u>John 15:19</u> - [19]*If ye were of the world, the world would love his own: but because ye are not of the world, but I have chosen you out of the world, therefore the world hateth you. (KJV)*

relate to the question he asked because having a Christian home and family is not popular.

It's been my observation that a lot of church-going families have children with more friends outside the church, or participate more in activities at their schools and in their communities than in their youth groups. There's nothing wrong in participating in school or civic activities, on the contrary these are good things, but our children shouldn't desire them more or put them before their activities within the church. Most often it's the church function that's cancelled without pause or consideration to meet the demands of the civic function. Should football practice fall on the same night as youth group, football usually wins. I agree we need to have something to attract the 'un-churched', but if after conversion they still need these things to stay in the church, something is wrong.

The Cost of Such a Decision

In [13]2 Corinthians 6:14-17 Paul now asks a question in the same spirit as Joshua and Elijah, asking the believer to make a choice. God interjected here in verse 17 commanding believers to *"come out from among them and be ye separate."* Contrary to Joshua and Elijah, this statement is New Testament, coming after Jesus died, resurrected and ascended, under the dispensation of the Holy Spirit. God is asking us to make a choice.

We must choose to come out from among the un-believer and be separate. We can't continue to flirt with the world and call ourselves Christian. We shouldn't have intimate relationships with people who don't know Jesus Christ as their personal Lord and Savior anymore. There should be a very distinctive and

---

[13] 2 Corinthians 6:14-17 - [14]*Be ye not unequally yoked together with unbelievers: for what fellowship hath righteousness with unrighteousness? and what communion hath light with darkness?* [15]*And what concord hath Christ with Belial? or what part hath he that believeth with an infidel?* [16]*And what agreement hath the temple of God with idols? for ye are the temple of the living God; as God hath said, I will dwell in them, and walk in them; and I will be their God, and they shall be my people.* [17]*Wherefore come out from among them, and be ye separate, saith the Lord, and touch not the unclean thing; and I will receive you.* (KJV)

precise difference between a true-believer and a non-believer. Just as light and darkness are two separate and distinguishable forces, so should a true-believer and non-believer.

In verses 14 and 15 this is how different we are supposed to be. This passage is in reference to the Old Testament pairing of a trained and submissive ox with a stubborn and free-willed donkey, which are different and difficult, and do not work together. It's a recipe for disaster. A true-believer plowing through life with a un-believer would be just as difficult. There will be two different characters fighting against each other. Our walk with God will be off at times, bringing confusion and indecision. Resistance is evident to living a Godly life when unequally yoked. This isn't just in reference to marriage, but every kind of relationship.

In verse [14]17 - the word *separate* in the Greek means to set off by boundary; to divide or sever. As a Christian I am going to have to set boundaries for me and my family. I'm going to have to make a choice not to go past those boundaries. If my friends are truly my

---

[14] 2 Corinthians 6:17 - [17]Wherefore come out from among them, and be ye separate, saith the Lord, and touch not the unclean thing; and I will receive you. (KJV)

As For Me & My House   Rev. Daniel L. Patrick

friends, they'll respect my decisions. They'll support my decision and walk with God, or else they'll turn around and leave. The word *touch* in the Greek means to attach one self, in other words - to fellowship or associate with in activity. And the word *unclean* in the Greek means morally impure, lewd or fowl. So the cost of serving God may be severing unfriendly attachments to those who are not believers, to say no to a party or get-together that isn't Godly, to stay away from people who entice us to compromise. We may have to keep our children home from an activity they want to participate that is immoral, socially or biblically wrong. We simply have to set our families away from the crowd.

God has so much to say about this in His Word. What is it to serve God? What did Joshua mean when he told the people *'choose you this day whom you will serve'*? I want to interject something here. When Joshua said, 'As for me and my house', he referred to himself first, and then he added his household. He didn't say, "I'll make my wife and children serve God, read their Bible and go to church, but I'll only do those things on occasion." No, he had to be the example, lead his household (his lineage of children, grandchildren, great-grandchildren) into obedience. He set a precedent in his house that God was God, and the only choice.

As for me and my house… we will serve the Lord. We are not going to vary, compromise or make excuses, whether it's popular or unpopular. I know by the words of Jesus that the world is going to persecute, detest and be hateful toward us for making this decision. If I'm walking this life without any resistance, I may be in compromise. That's a powerful thought.

In conclusion, the only thing that matters is my relationship with God through Jesus Christ our Lord.

Chapter 2

The Difference between Men & Women

In [15]Joshua 24:14-15, Joshua included his self first and then spoke for his family when he declared, *"But as for me and my house, we will serve the Lord."* He didn't sit down with his wife, children and even servants and ask for a vote. As the spiritual and responsible head of his family, he boldly proclaimed what his family would do. This whole book revolves around family relationships, and in this chapter I'm going to focus mainly on the subtle differences between the roles of men and women.

We all know or have learned early in life that men and women are different. There are very obvious differences that need no debate. However, in this

---

[15] *Joshua 24:14-15* -[14]*Now therefore fear the LORD, and serve him in sincerity and in truth: and put away the gods which your fathers served on the other side of the flood, and in Egypt; and serve ye the LORD.* [15]*And if it seem evil unto you to serve the LORD, choose you this day whom ye will serve; whether the gods which your fathers served that were on the other side of the flood, or the gods of the Amorites, in whose land ye dwell: but as for me and my house, we will serve the LORD. (KJV)*

chapter I'm going to focus more on those subtle differences that aren't so obvious, and usually ignored or un-discussed.

To say the least, there's been an on-going war between the sexes; a fight for equality and in some cases supremacy. Both fights are fought in vain, because we are already equal. The struggle isn't about who is superior, because superiority isn't in question. It's not about a man being superior to a woman, and a woman being inferior to the man. It's not about a man being inferior to the woman, and a woman being superior to a man. We've got to change our mindsets. It's not about superiority or inferiority… it's about the order of God.

In the corporate world, before a product is produced, its function is already established. It would be absurd and useless to design a product without a function in mind. Male and female were designed with a particular function and purpose.

The Designer

In [16]Genesis 1:27 we learn that God created us, both male and female. We didn't create ourselves, God created us. We are His creation. When created, our function and purpose was already known. God didn't create us just because He could; He created us with a purpose in mind.

In [17]Genesis 2:18 God says it's not good for man to be alone. In other words, God knew the man needed help, and so with a purpose God made him a help-meet. God's purpose and plan could not be fulfilled without both male and female, who were joined together to make things complete. The word ***help-meet*** in the Hebrew means one who completes; completer. Again, our existence is not about superiority or inferiority; it's about function and order. We need to get back to this basic principle in order for our lives and homes to function properly.

---

[16] <u>Genesis 1:27</u> - [27]*So God created man in his own image, in the image of God created he him; male and female created he them. (KJV)*

[17] <u>Genesis 2:18</u> - [18]*And the LORD God said, It is not good that the man should be alone; I will make him an help meet for him. (KJV)*

I say to myself, "God made me. I not only have a purpose, but I was created for a purpose!"

Illustration: I hold a hammer and tape measure in my hand. Which is the most dominate? Which is more superior? What word or category would fit both objects? Most would say, 'tool'. Which of these 'tools' are superior or more dominate, and why?

The answer is neither. Although the hammer could crush the tape measure, both tools are needed to build the house. They need each other, though with different functions, to fulfill the same purpose. In the building of the house they are not useful without the other. What good is a measured board without a hammer to fasten it to its proper place? What good is a hammer without a measured board to place? We can then reason that neither superiority nor inferiority is in question. They are doing what they were designed and purposed to do - complete the job.

It's the enemy's job to disrupt the order of God when it comes to men and women. God designed us to work together, not separate. Jesus said, "[18]*Every house divided against its self shall not stand.*" The enemy wants men and women, husbands and wives, brothers and sisters to stay at odds with each other so they cannot fulfill their purpose and stay out of the order God created.

Before the designer of the measuring tape made it, he sat down and contemplated its purpose. Before the hammer was forged, the maker knew what it looked like and what functions it had. Before God created us, He already predestined our function and purpose. There are households today that are out of order, who've allowed the enemy to come in and change the roles from which God intended.

The Design

In [19]Genesis 1:28 God tells us we (man and woman) were designed to be fruitful and multiply,

---

[18] Matthew 12:25 - *And Jesus knew their thoughts, and said unto them,* **Every** *kingdom* **divided** *against itself is brought to desolation; and* **every** *city or* **house** **divided** *against itself shall not stand: (KJV)*

[19] Genesis 1:28 - [28]*And God blessed them, and God said unto them, Be fruitful, and multiply, and replenish the earth, and subdue it: and have dominion over the fish of the sea, and over the fowl of the air, and over every living thing that moveth upon the earth. (KJV)*

replenish the earth and subdue it and have dominion over it. The word *subdue* in the Hebrew means to conquer or bring into subjection. The word *dominion* in the Hebrew means to reign or rule over. Men and women were to do this together, not alone. The female was given equal authority as the man. God did not differentiate between them. To be fruitful, multiply, replenish, subdue and dominate wasn't a one-man job, and couldn't be achieved separately. It took both, man and woman, working together.

God also commanded the couple to be fruitful and multiply, to reproduce. Reproduction requires action and contribution of both male and female, sperm and egg, and it cannot be processed alone. However, here being fruitful and multiplying didn't just refer to the physical, but more importantly to the spiritual. God does care who you marry. He does care who you start a family or join yourself with. That's why it's important for Christian moms and dads to pray hard for their children *before* they get married, that the right person would come into their life. God commanded them to produce a family. Households built on God's Word have the power to subdue and take dominion over sickness, poverty, or any other thing the enemy brings against it. But, the physical and spiritual design can only happen if the man and woman work together. Our spiritual walk is not about superiority or dominion; it's about the order of God.

The Difference

Now, I want to focus on the differences between men and women. After the fall from being disobedient and eating the forbidden fruit, God dealt with men and women differently and independently. There's a difference of accountability for men and women. I want to first address the woman.

In [20]Genesis 3:16 God declares that the woman was to bear children and her sorrow was to be multiplied. The word *sorrow* in the Hebrew means worrisome. Here God did not just refer to physical pain, but also emotional pain. Have you ever noticed how a mother feels toward her children is different than a father? It's no coincidence; it's God's design. Mother's

---

[20] Genesis 3:16 - [16]Unto the woman he said, I will greatly multiply thy sorrow and thy conception; in sorrow thou shalt bring forth children; and thy desire shall be to thy husband, and he shall rule over thee. (KJV)

are more affectionate, gentle and understanding as a general rule. For the most part, children run to their mother's for comfort more than their fathers. Why do you think that is? It's the design of a woman. Because the woman is more sensitive, they are also more troubled and experience more sorrow; in layman's terms - more emotional. For instance, a man wants to take the bull by the horn, while the woman shows concern, even for the bull.

We are different, yet equal. Never be ashamed of how God made you or who you are. You're not inferior because you look different. Each sex has their own strengths and weaknesses and they think differently from one another, just like we humans think differently from God. Most often times, women are emotionally stronger, while men are physically stronger.

In [21]Proverbs 29:15 Solomon declares that a child left to them self brings a mother to shame. Why only a mother and not a mother and father? This is an example of the grief and sorrow that a woman

---

[21] Proverbs 29:15 - [15]*The rod and reproof give wisdom: but a child left to himself bringeth his mother to shame. (KJV)*

As For Me & My House · Rev. Daniel L. Patrick

experiences. It's not that a man doesn't care the same as a woman, but he responds differently.

In Genesis 3:16, God declared that a woman's desire would be for her husband. The word *desire* in the Hebrew means, a longing; a yearning. So, another difference is for the woman to have the desire for the man. Why this is so may be explained in the next verse.

In [22]Genesis 3:17 God spoke to Adam and said, *"...because thou hearkened unto the voice of thy wife..."* Adam obeyed his wife and disobeyed God by eating from the tree. Let's look at this a moment. Is the Word of God coming against the woman, or the disobedience of the man, or both? We see several principles here:

- God spoke to Adam
- Woman spoke to Adam
- Women have power over men at times, even when it comes to obeying God

---

[22] <u>Genesis 3:17</u> - [17]*And unto Adam he said, Because thou hast hearkened unto the voice of thy wife, and hast eaten of the tree, of which I commanded thee, saying, Thou shalt not eat of it: cursed is the ground for thy sake; in sorrow shalt thou eat of it all the days of thy life; (KJV)*

Notice also that God cursed the ground and not the man, saying, *"cursed is the ground for thy sake; in **sorrow*** (which in the Hebrew means toil and pain) *shall thou eat of it all the days of thy life."*

The consequence for the woman because of sin is pain and sorrow after child birth and for her desire to be after the man, because he has the rule over her. The word ***rule*** in the Hebrew means to have dominion, to govern or to have power over.

The consequence for the man because of sin is to labor and work for what God had freely given him before he sinned. This isn't all man is required to do, and this doesn't mean women are to become a slave to them.

The differences between men and women go so much deeper than a physical appearance. Both have a purpose and neither is greater than the other. Who we are as a human is about knowing our spiritual make-up. It's about knowing our purpose.

Chapter 3

The Spiritual Responsibilities of a Man

Up to this point we have learned what it is to serve God, and the difference between men and women. In chapter two I wanted to stress that God didn't make man as the superior over the woman, but he blessed them (together), gave them dominion, and told them to subdue. It's a joint effort to accomplish what God has ordained. So, I want to re-iterate that it's not about superiority or inferiority, but about God's order. In this chapter I want you to discover that our spiritual responsibilities as a man and woman work together to achieve what God has planned for us, but also showcase the differences. The spiritual responsibility of a man is not the same as the spiritual responsibility of a woman.

We are His Workmanship

In [23]Ephesians 2:10 we discover that 'we' are 'His' workmanship. Remember from Chapter 2 we

---

[23] _Ephesians 2:10_ - *10For we are his workmanship, created in Christ Jesus unto good works, which God hath before ordained that we should walk in them. (KJV)*

learned that the purpose of a product is pre-determined before it is produced. God created us; we are His workmanship, and we were created unto "good works'. These good works were known before we were created.

In the second half of this scripture we see '*which God hath before ordained*', before what? Before we were created, God had a purpose for us. The word **ordain** in the Greek means to fit up in advance or prepare before. So, another tidbit we must remember is that God's plan has not changed and the spiritual responsibilities of men and women were already set before they were created. Just as the responsibilities were made before we were made, God expected us to walk in them even before we could walk. The word **walk** in the Greek means to live; to deport oneself to. So, in general, we share the same spiritual responsibility – to live Godly lives.

Man's Spiritual Responsibility

In [24]Genesis 3:1-7 the serpent came to the woman. Now this is very interesting because he spoke only to the woman. Maybe, just maybe, the serpent knew the order of God. The serpent reminded Eve of what God had said to Adam, so we can conclude here that Eve knew the commandment of God. But, Eve listened to the serpent and looked at the tree and it didn't look evil. Matter of fact, it was a very beautiful tree. As the serpent told her, it would even make her smarter. What's wrong with that? She didn't see any fault in the serpent's reasoning and she took the fruit and ate it. Then, after she'd eaten it herself, took some of it and gave it to Adam. Perhaps seeing no immediate response to disobedience, Adam too ate of the fruit.

---

[24] <u>Genesis 3:1-7</u> - *¹Now the serpent was more subtle than any beast of the field which the LORD God had made. And he said unto the woman, Yea, hath God said, Ye shall not eat of every tree of the garden? ²And the woman said unto the serpent, We may eat of the fruit of the trees of the garden: ³But of the fruit of the tree which is in the midst of the garden, God hath said, Ye shall not eat of it, neither shall ye touch it, lest ye die. ⁴And the serpent said unto the woman, Ye shall not surely die: ⁵For God doth know that in the day ye eat thereof, then your eyes shall be opened, and ye shall be as gods, knowing good and evil. ⁶And when the woman saw that the tree was good for food, and that it was pleasant to the eyes, and a tree to be desired to make one wise, she took of the fruit thereof, and did eat, and gave also unto her husband with her; and he did eat. ⁷And the eyes of them both were opened, and they knew that they were naked; and they sewed fig leaves together, and made themselves aprons.* (KJV)

What I find astonishing is that it wasn't until after Adam ate the forbidden fruit that both of their eyes were opened. Why was Eve's eyes not opened after she alone ate the forbidden fruit? The word, *eyes,* in the Hebrew means knowledge or vision. After Adam ate the fruit, they both (together) now knew they were naked.

We may have been reading a different story today if Adam, the man, would have resisted the temptation and took control of the situation, instead of being disobedient.

In [25]Exodus 20:5 the Word says that God visits the iniquities of the father's upon the children. Let's look at three words here. The first word *visiting* in the Hebrew means to visit with either friendly or hostile intent; to hurt; or do judgment. The second word *iniquity* in the Hebrew means perversity, moral evil or sin. The last word *father* in the Hebrew means either immediate father or father's father (grandfather).

Let's think about this for a moment. Sin comes to visit our family members to the third and fourth

---

[25] Exodus 20:5 - ⁵*Thou shalt not bow down thyself to them, nor serve them: for I the LORD thy God am a jealous God, visiting the iniquity of the fathers upon the children unto the third and fourth generation of them that hate me; (KJV)*

generation, and it comes through the man, not the woman. God holds the man responsible for the sin that's not dealt with in a family. It's not the woman's responsibility. It's her responsibility to be a Godly woman, but it's the man who allows sin to be passed down through the generations, commonly known as 'generational' curses. By the same token, it is through the man in which 'generational blessings' are also passed down.

[26]Romans 5:12-15 supports evidence of the responsibilities of man. In verse 12 – *'wherefore as by one man'* the word **man** in the Greek means a male human being. So, according to this scripture it was by one male, Adam, that sin entered the world. Wait, didn't Eve eat the forbidden fruit first? She was the one who started it, and the one who the serpent enticed, yet here the Apostle Paul clearly defines Adam as the guilty

---

[26] *Romans 5:12-15* - [12]*Wherefore, as by one man sin entered into the world, and death by sin; and so death passed upon all men, for that all have sinned:* [13]*(For until the law sin was in the world: but sin is not imputed when there is no law.* [14]*Nevertheless death reigned from Adam to Moses, even over them that had not sinned after the similitude of Adam's transgression, who is the figure of him that was to come.* [15]*But not as the offence, so also is the free gift. For if through the offence of one many be dead, much more the grace of God, and the gift by grace, which is by one man, Jesus Christ, hath abounded unto many. (KJV)*

culprit. Maybe Eve did eat the forbidden fruit first, but perhaps God expected the man Adam to stop it. It was his responsibility to keep iniquity from his family, not hers.

In verse 15 – *'by one man the gift of grace was give to us all.'* Are you getting this yet? It's not about male or female, it's about who God holds responsible. This is why Jesus was born a male, not because man is greater than woman, but because God holds the man responsible. The 'man' Adam sinned, so the 'man' Christ had to make it right. Christ re-established man's authority and responsibility.

In [27]verse 19 – *'For as by one man's disobedience many were made sinners, so by the obedience of one shall many be made righteous.'* We cannot have the authority of the man without the responsibility of the man. You cannot have the responsibility of the man unless you are a man. This is where the serpent still tries to upset the order of God. We sometimes equate authority with superiority. It

---

[27] <u>Romans 5:19</u> - [19]*For as by one man's disobedience many were made sinners, so by the obedience of one shall many be made righteous. (KJV)*

seems the more authority someone has, they more superior they become, but this is not the case.

In [28]Genesis 3:16 *'and he shall rule over thee'*, God meant for the man to have authority and responsibility over the woman. This goes back to Ephesians 2:10 and the revelation that God made us, He designed us for a purpose, and He gave each (man & woman) of us a physical and spiritual design. He did this because He wanted us to do His will. The man is the one held responsible for the welfare of his family, both spiritually and physically.

---

[28] Genesis 3:16 - [16]*Unto the woman he said, I will greatly multiply thy sorrow and thy conception; in sorrow thou shalt bring forth children; and thy desire shall be to thy husband, and he shall rule over thee. (KJV)*

Chapter 4

The Spiritual Responsibilities of a Woman

In the last chapter we learned that the man was responsible and accountable to God for his family, and that the husband has been given rule over the wife, as stated in [29]Genesis 3:16. In this chapter I want to now focus on the woman's responsibility and the design and plan God intended for women. Remember, we've already learned that this book isn't about superiority or inferiority, but about the order of God. We also learned in the last chapter that the woman ate the forbidden fruit first, but the man was held accountable.

God's Plan for Women

As we take a closer look at Genesis 3:16, the first judgment was that her sorrow would be greatly multiplied. Then, at the end of the scripture we learned that her husband would have rule over her. Now, notice

---

[29] *Genesis 3:16* - *[16]Unto the woman he said, I will greatly multiply thy sorrow and thy conception; in sorrow thou shalt bring forth children; and thy desire shall be to thy husband, and he shall rule over thee. (KJV)*

here that God didn't declare this judgment onto Eve alone and individually, but pronounced it upon the 'woman' in general, and then in the later part onto the 'wife' as God mentioned 'husband' and not 'man'. Nowhere does this scripture indicate that men in general were to have rule over women in general, though that is often how it is interpreted. It only states that a woman was to have great sorrow in childbirth and that as a wife her desire would be for her husband, and her husband would rule over her.

Also in this scripture we can only come to the conclusion that Adam told Eve what God had told him concerning the law as noted in Genesis 2:16. It was to man in which God commanded not to eat from the tree, therefore making Eve disobedient to man.

Let's take a closer look at Genesis 3:16 when God said to the woman that her desire was to be to thy husband, and he shall rule over her. The word *desire* in the Hebrew means longing. And the word *rule* in the Hebrew means to have dominion, to govern, or to have power over. At first glance, this statement might upset women, but I want to couple it with the spiritual responsibilities of a man. If God is holding the man accountable, it would only stand to reason He would give man the rule. This doesn't mean that men should boss women around, nor does it imply to abuse this authority or rule, because the woman is an equal partner. Remember, God gave 'them' dominion over the earth, but God gave man to rule over the woman. This is a joint effort; both being what God intended.

In [30]Genesis 2:18 God declared that is was not good that man should be alone. This was God's observation, not mans. God didn't make Adam and then ask Adam what he (Adam) wanted or thought; God declared himself that it was not good for Adam to be alone. So, the idea of a woman coming after a man was God's.

The word *good* in the Hebrew means pleasant, well or pleasing. So, when God made Adam, He (God) said it is not pleasant, well or pleasing that 'the' man (Adam) should be alone. The word *alone* in the Hebrew means just a part; as in a branch on a tree; to be solitary.

---

[30] <u>Genesis 2:18</u> - *[18]And the LORD God said, It is not good that the man should be alone; I will make him an help meet for him. (KJV)*

Let's look a little closer. The fact may be that the woman wasn't made for the man's pleasure, or one person to have authority over the other. The fact here may be that God saw that His (God's) plan couldn't be carried out with just the man alone. Therefore, God said, "I will make him a help-meet for him." The word **help** in the Hebrew means to aid; protect. The word **meet** in the Hebrew means a counterpart or mate.

The question is: "Was woman made for man or just from man?" Or, "Was woman made because God saw that man couldn't carry out His (God's) plan alone?" Once again, this lesson isn't about superiority, it's about the order of God. I can only conclude that God's plan for the woman was to assist the man in carrying out the plans of God.

In [31]Proverbs 19:21, the Word declares – *"There are many devices in a man's heart; nevertheless the counsel of the LORD, that shall stand."* What does this mean? I believe it means that there are many ways we can go, many things we can do, but it's what God has ordained for us to do that really matters.

---

[31] *Proverbs 19:21* - [21]*There are many devices in a man's heart; nevertheless the counsel of the LORD, that shall stand. (KJV)*

I have heard most of my life that a woman's place is in the home. I've also heard that a woman's place is anywhere a man can go. The world screams, "Equal Rights!" But, the Bible says that the spiritual responsibilities and rights are God-given. Culture and tradition have established distorted views of the roles of men and women. Most women today have obtained their identities from worldly teachers and philosophers, rather than God. Because of the misuse and abuse that women have endured - God's purpose in their lives have greatly been damaged. It is God's plan that needs to be understood.

Women are not, nor have ever been, lesser vessels. Women are just vessels with different functions than men. This "function" is just as important, regardless of its difference. It's not until we (humans) fully embrace the truth of God's Word, that we will value ourselves as God values us.

The Virtuous Woman

Proverbs 31:30 – *30"Favour is deceitful, and beauty is vain: but a woman that feareth the LORD, she shall be praised."* In other words, a woman who reverently and worshipfully fears the Lord shall be praised.

Proverbs 31:11 – *"The heart of her husband doth safely trust in her, so that he shall have no need of spoil."* In other words, a woman should have the trust of her husband.

Proverbs 31:15 - *"She riseth also while it is yet night, and giveth meat to her household, and a portion to her maidens."* In other words, she rises early to get spiritual food for her family, she prays, she seeks God for direction for herself and her family. This shows that the woman also prays for the family, not just the man. I'd advise, women don't throw all your prayers onto the shoulders of your husbands. Go to your husbands and share with him what God has given you in prayer. However, don't say, "This is what you are to do!" Allow your husbands, through their own prayer, to make the right decisions.

Proverbs 31:21 – *"She is not afraid of the snow for her household: for all her household are clothed with scarlet."* What does it mean that she's not afraid of the snow? The word, **snow** in the Hebrew means to be pure like snow; white. What does 'her household is clothed in scarlet' mean? In the book of Genesis, it means being marked for inheritance. In the book of Joshua it refers to scarlet as protection. In the book of Exodus, it refers to earthly glory. Scarlet was also used in the customs of the Tabernacle and used on the cloth that covers the entrance to the Holy of Holies. In II Samuel, scarlet suggests prosperity. In Leviticus, it means purification. In Numbers, it was to recognize the coming of Christ and His redemption.

Remember, we're not talking about a man here, but a woman. Can you imagine, as a woman, your spiritual position allows you to clothe your household in purification, redemption, prosperity, access to God, earthly glory, protection and last but certainly not least… marking your family for inheritance? It doesn't say men do this, but women.

In Proverbs 31:22-33 – *"She maketh herself coverings of tapestry; her clothing is silk and purple"*.

Clothes of tapestry, silk and purple are clothes worn by the priests of the Temple. In other words, a woman knows who she is in the Lord. *"Her husband is known in*

the gates, when he sitteth among the elders of the land."
A virtuous woman makes her husband look good in the sight of others. I cannot say enough about this! When a woman knows who she is in Christ, she's not in a power struggle with her husband, but realizes how vitally important their spiritual responsibilities are. They not only bless their family and others around them, they bless God.

The spiritual responsibility of a woman is equally as valuable as that of a man. The only difference is... they're different.

Chapter 5

The Sanctity of Marriage

The word *Sanctity* means sacredness, holiness, purity; the state of being consecrated to a deity. Anything held sacred. We as born-again believers need to regard marriage as sacred, not just a ceremony we are expected to go through in front of people, but as a sacred institution ordained and originated by God. Marriage is to be taken with the utmost awareness of its true meaning.

The world's philosophy of marriage is a far cry from what God intended it to be. People often fly in and out of marriages with little to no idea of its true meaning. There are so-called 'starter marriages' where people enter into marriage with the idea that if things don't work out, they can just try again. This is not what God intended, to say the least. He wanted man and woman to be joined together until death. God doesn't know 'starter marriages'. God understands everything, but His understanding doesn't constitute His acceptance.

It's true – divorce happens. But, if marriage was entered into with the mindset of "I'm in love and I'm going to do what God expects me to do to make this marriage work", there would be less divorce.

The First Marriage

[32]Genesis 2:24 – God caused Adam to fall into a deep sleep, took one of his ribs, closed up the flesh and then from the rib made a woman. Man had absolutely nothing to do with the creation of the woman. In fact, man didn't even have a say in it. It was all God's doing. After God made the woman, God brought her to the man. It was only then did Adam have any kind of say. Let's now take a look at what he said.

In verse 23, Adam said, *"This is now bone of my bones and flesh of my flesh; she shall be called Woman, because she was taken out of Man."*

---

[32] Genesis 2:21-24 – [21]*And the LORD God caused a deep sleep to fall upon Adam, and he slept: and he took one of his ribs, and closed up the flesh instead thereof;* [22]*And the rib, which the LORD God had taken from man, made he a woman, and brought her unto the man.* [23]*And Adam said, This is now bone of my bones, and flesh of my flesh: she shall be called Woman, because she was taken out of Man.* [24]*Therefore shall a man leave his father and his mother, and shall cleave unto his wife: and they shall be one flesh. (KJV)*

Bone of my bone in the Hebrew means a extension of the body; self-same body. ***Flesh of my flesh*** in the Hebrew means same kin or kind. ***Woman*** in the Hebrew means of man; man with a womb or female man. Adam said she was taken from Man, not she was taken from me. The point being that Adam knew God's plan and that he was only one part of it, the beginning of it, and not the complete plan on his own. This is a great example of Adam being submissive to his Creator.

In verse 24, the Bible says, *"Therefore shall a man leave his father and mother and shall cleave unto his wife; and they two shall become one flesh."* Marriage was the first institution established up on the earth. The three laws or rules of the marriage bond are:

1. <u>There is to be a leaving of the parents.</u> This separation from the parents means that the relationship between husband and wife should be stronger than between parent and child. It's not that parental guidance should be ignored after marriage, but that the love and companionship of husband and wife should be stronger. The covenant of marriage

between a man and woman is to be more durable than parent and child.

2. <u>There is to be a cleaving to each other</u>. The word *cleave* in the Hebrew means to join fast together; to glue together; to be joined in the closest union possible; to be inseparable. The idea here is that only ones that are to leave a family are the children, and they should leave to get married. The union of marriage was ordained by God to be stronger than the union of parent and child.

3. <u>There is to be one flesh</u>. The word *flesh* in the Hebrew means same kin or kind. The husband belongs to the wife. The wife belongs to the husband. They are to be as one person. There are three unions within a marriage: physical, mental and most of all spiritual. It is God yoking, God binding, God joining the couple together into a spiritual union that causes them to be one person.

Marriages of Today

Let's look at [33]I Timothy 4:1-3 in the context of marriage. *"Now the Spirit (Holy Spirit) speaketh expressly"*. The word ***expressly*** in the Hebrew means manifestly or openly. *"...That in the later times some shall depart from 'the' faith, giving heed to seducing spirits, and doctrines of devils."*

We live in a time where some people are hunting for churches that don't challenge their lifestyle, hunting for doctrines and teachings that make them feel good about their disobedience to God, and this is the same for the institution of marriage.

We can develop a perverted sense of security because of God's goodness. We can also develop a mindset that thinks because God is good there is no repercussion for our disobedience. If we're not careful we can become de-sensitized to God's Holy Spirit and

---

[33] <u>1 Timothy 4:1-3</u> – *[1]Now the Spirit speaketh expressly, that in the latter times some shall depart from the faith, giving heed to seducing spirits, and doctrines of devils; [2]Speaking lies in hypocrisy; having their conscience seared with a hot iron; [3]Forbidding to marry, and commanding to abstain from meats, which God hath created to be received with thanksgiving of them which believe and know the truth.* (KJV)

conform to the age in which we live. The original purpose and design for marriage seems to be foolish to some people. Its sacredness and holiness are soon too quickly forgotten as with the vows of marriage.

Marriage Vows

Marriage is a sacred institution, the basis of human society, and should be held in high honor among all men and women. We are assembled here in the presence of God to join this man and this woman in holy marriage, which is instituted of God and regulated by His holy commandments, and blessed by our Lord, Jesus Christ. Let us therefore reverently remember that God has established and sanctified marriage for the welfare of happiness of mankind. Our Savior has declared that a man shall leave his father and mother and cleave unto his wife. By His Apostles, He has instructed those of us who have entered into this relationship to cherish in mutual esteem and love, to bear with each other's infirmities and weaknesses; to comfort each other in sickness, trouble and sorrow; To provide for each other and for their household in temporal things; to pray for and encourage each other in the things pertaining to God; To live together as heirs of His grace.

Man, do you solemnly agree before God and these witnesses, to take this woman to be your lawful wedded wife, to love and respect her, honor and cherish her in health and in sicknesses, in prosperity and in adversity, and in leaving all others to keep yourself only unto her as long as you both shall live?

Woman, do you in like-manner solemnly to agree to receive this man as your lawfully wedded husband, to love and respect him, to live with him in all faith and tenderness, in health and in sickness, in prosperity and in adversity, and leaving all others to keep yourself only unto him as long as you both shall live?

This oath, promise and covenant is made before witnesses and with the opening statement that 'we are assembled in the presence of God', standing before the Creator who made us, and standing before the One who declared how marriage should be.

Marriages of today need to hold fast to the principles and precepts of the first marriage. The last poll about marriage states that fifty-percent of all marriages end in divorce. Divorce in some cases is inevitable, but I don't think divorce should happen as often as it does. Marriage is sacred, holy and pure. It is the joining of a man and woman together as God intended. A blessed marriage is a Godly marriage.

[34]Mark 10:7-9 represents the new covenant writing concerning marriage. The word *asunder* in the Greek means to put room between; separate. Marriage never originated as a law of man, nor should it be viewed that way. It originated by God to be between a man and a woman. Marriage in the sight of God is not just two people living together and signing a contract, it's a union ordained and purposed by God. It's a man and woman living for each other under God, acknowledging God in every way. Any union not ordained or sanctioned by God isn't by definition

---

[34] Mark 10:7-9 – [7]*For this cause shall a man leave his father and mother, and cleave to his wife;* [8]*And they twain shall be one flesh: so then they are no more twain, but one flesh.* [9]*What therefore God hath joined together, let not man put asunder. (KJV)*

marriage. In the current political arena, our courts are trying to redefine the definition of marriage in order to satisfy a cry for an institution not sanctioned by God, departing from 'the' faith, and heeding to the voice of worldly persuasion. Changing the worldly definition of something doesn't make it acceptable by God. God defines marriage, not man.

Marriage requires work. Never will we get to the place where we can just lay back and tip-toe through the tulips. Husbands and wives will always have to set their minds on the things of God. They should always learn how to be better husbands and wives. God never promised a smooth marriage. There are going to be problem areas that may take years to conquer, but don't give up on each other. Mostly, don't count the power of God short in your marriage. Take a stand and say, *"As for me and my house, we will serve the Lord."*

Chapter 6

The Responsibilities of Husband & Wife

Up until this point we've studied about the responsibilities of men and women, but now we are going to go a little further and get a little more specific, especially in the area of husbands and wives. Not every man is a husband. Not every woman is a wife.

God's Word is very specific about marriage and the roles of husbands and wives. I would even go so far as to say that a family, children included, cannot function properly unless the husband and wife walk according to the Word. There is no way that children can be raised properly unless the husband and wife relationship is following God's Word. God never varies from His order. He works from the top down.

I know we've all heard sermons and teachings on husbands and wives, but for some reason and in some cases God's order is not 'applied' to the marriage. It's not enough to know what to do; we must fight our flesh and walk in God's Word. I will reiterate once again that this walk is not about superiority, but about the order of God.

Headship

In [35]I Corinthians 11:3, Paul starts this letter by saying, *"I would have you to know."* In other words, if we don't understand headships and see it as an authoritative position and not as a position of superiority, we will not recognize nor submit to it. The word **know** in the Greek means to perceive; to be aware of; to look on. It's more than a mechanical or passive vision; but one of intense observation and continued inspection. The word **head** in the Greek means a part most readily taken hold of. The head of every man is Christ. The word **man** in the Greek means an individual male, fellow or husband. It also comes from another Greek word meaning man-faced or human being. So, it's clear that Paul was referring to a human male in this scripture. It goes on to differentiate when it states that the head of the woman is man, and the head of Christ is God.

---

[35] *1 Corinthians 11:3* - ³*But I would have you know, that the head of every man is Christ; and the head of the woman is the man; and the head of Christ is God. (KJV)*

Can you see the order that has been established? This is not man's order, but God's order. No one else has a say in it, regardless of opinion, cultural acceptance or political correctness. God always operates in order, but we may not sometimes. God is the same yesterday, today and forever.

In [36]Ephesians 5:23 we see a repeat of what we just learned in 1 Corinthians 11:3 that the man is the head of the woman, except this time it's more specific to husband and wife. But, it doesn't stop there. It goes on to say, *"That even as Christ is the head of the church..."* The word *even* in the Greek means likewise. So, like Christ, who is the Savior of the body (church), the husband must be the same toward and over his wife. We must understand that Paul related this to the function of the church and headship in reference to the 'position' of authority. The head of our natural body controls the functions of the body; however it would never lead it or cause it to do anything to harm itself (being in its right mind, of course). So, just as Christ leads the church, the husband is to lead the wife.

---

[36] *Ephesians 5:23* - *[23]For the husband is the head of the wife, even as Christ is the head of the church: and he is the saviour of the body. (KJV)*

Submission

Here is where things get a little touchy. If we back up one verse and look at [37]Ephesians 5:22 we see that wives are to submit to their husbands. We may ask, "Why does the woman have to do all the submitting?" The answer is... they don't. We've got to go back one more verse in [38]Ephesians 5:21 to see that we (Christian believers – including both husbands and wives) are to submit to one another.

Let's take a closer look at this. The scripture says, *"Wives submit yourselves unto your own husbands."* Not every man, just your husbands. However, we are to treat everyone with respect. Here the Bible doesn't teach that women are under the authority of men, but that wives are under the authority of their own husbands. There is a great difference between the two. However, the passage goes on to describe how this submission is to be... *"As unto the Lord."*

---

[37] <u>Ephesians 5:22</u> - *[22]Wives, submit yourselves unto your own husbands, as unto the Lord. (KJV)*

[38] <u>Ephesians 5:21</u> - *[21]Submitting yourselves one to another in the fear of God. (KJV)*

The phrase '*as unto the Lord*' means when we do anything, we are to do it as if we were doing it for the Lord. It's not that the husband is worthy, but the Lord. When wives submit themselves unto their husbands, it's because the Lord has asked them. By pleasing the husband, the wife pleases the Lord.

Ephesians 5:24 doesn't mean that wives are to obey their husbands no matter what happens, but to obey in all lawful and right things. None of us, including wives, should do anything illegal, immoral or goes against Scripture because God and His commandments come first. This should go without saying, but if either spouse is a believer, the true believer is to live a Godly life before their spouse without compromise to the Word.

The Love of the Husband

Now it's time to focus on the husband. In [39]Ephesians 5:25, husbands are to love their wives, even as Christ also loved the church and gave Himself for it. The word *love* in the Greek means agape. The love in

---

[39] Ephesians 5:25 - *25Husbands, love your wives, even as Christ also loved the church, and gave himself for it; (KJV)*

which a husband is to love his wife is with the very love that is God. It's a selfless, unselfish love; one that gives and sacrifices. It's not just a love of feelings and emotions, but one of a strong will and commitment.

Think about this for a moment. How does Christ love the church? He loves us when we don't deserve it and He loves us even if we aren't worthy. He loves us when we turn our backs on Him. He loves us even if we walk in disobedience to Him. Christ has committed and willed to love us even unto death. This is the love a husband is to have for his wife. I would add that if husbands would love their wives this way, there wouldn't be any issue with submission.

Christ brings the church to him by love and compassion, not through fear or manipulation. The point here is a real eye-opener. It brings out that the success of marriage is based on the love of the husband. The love of a husband has a great effect on the marriage. Few wives could or would reject a love that was selfless and sacrificial. A marriage based on this kind of love will be a strong and long-lasting.

So, when Paul exhorted the wife to submit, he also told the husband how to love. The point being, it was never meant to be a one-sided relationship. On the flip side, one-sided disobedience in a marriage doesn't give the spouse permission, or a right, to also be disobedient.

In [40]1 Peter 3:1-7 we discover that a disobedient husband can be won by the obedience of the faith-filled wife. We need to be careful what we say. More arguments are started by 'using' the Word of God, rather than 'doing' the Word of God. Christ didn't come to preach to us; He came to love us.

In verse 3 we discover that women need to be careful of trying to win men with their appearance or

---

[40] *1 Peter 3:1-7* - *¹Likewise, ye wives, be in subjection to your own husbands; that, if any obey not the word, they also may without the word be won by the conversation of the wives; ²While they behold your chaste conversation coupled with fear. ³Whose adorning let it not be that outward adorning of plaiting the hair, and of wearing of gold, or of putting on of apparel; ⁴But let it be the hidden man of the heart, in that which is not corruptible, even the ornament of a meek and quiet spirit, which is in the sight of God of great price. ⁵For after this manner in the old time the holy women also, who trusted in God, adorned themselves, being in subjection unto their own husbands: ⁶Even as Sara obeyed Abraham, calling him lord: whose daughters ye are, as long as ye do well, and are not afraid with any amazement. ⁷Likewise, ye husbands, dwell with them according to knowledge, giving honour unto the wife, as unto the weaker vessel, and as being heirs together of the grace of life; that your prayers be not hindered. (KJV)*

physical attractiveness. This may work for a while, but a marriage can't survive on this alone. It's the beauty of the soul that really matters. I've see outward beauty with no inward beauty, and it makes the whole body ugly. Yes it's true we live in a superficial world. But, we are not of this world, and we are to know the person we marry.

In verse 7 we discover that if a household is not built on God's Word it's in trouble. If the husband doesn't give honor unto the wife, and see her as a joint heir of God, then the prayers of that household are hindered. The word **honor** in the Greek means to value; to esteem to the highest degree. The word **hindered** in the Greek means to frustrate; to cut down or cut off. The spiritual and physical welfare of a marriage hinges on the relationship of the husband and wife, and most of all on their relationship with God. As for me and my house, we will serve the Lord.

Chapter 7

Parental Duty

When Joshua made the statement, *"As for me and my house"*, he was making a very broad and bold statement. The word ***house*** in the Hebrew means family and/or dwelling. In essence, Joshua said, "my family, my children and my lineage will serve the Lord." It was a decision of determination and dedication.

Another aspect when Joshua made this declaration is the fact he involved himself first... *"as for Me"*. He knew the importance of being the spiritual leader of his family. He knew that it wouldn't be enough to stand behind his family's decision to serve God, but it was for him to lead them in service to God.

In the age we live in, it is difficult to raise children and be a family that serves God. I've said this time and time again. It's not at all popular with or in your workplace, it is not popular for your children in schools and it's surely not popular in today's society as a whole. But, God knows this and has given us instructions on how to raise our children and be a Godly home. This hasn't changed.

What is it to train up a child?

[41]Proverbs 22:6 is a very familiar passage of scripture. It begins, *"Train up a child..."* Let's look at some of the words here. The word **train** in the Hebrew means narrow, imitate, discipline and to dedicate. It also comes from another Hebrew word meaning to choke. The word **child** in the Hebrew means the age of infancy to adolescence. The word **way** in the Hebrew here means the road or course of life; mode of action.

Wow, how dynamic are these words? These are not passive words, but active action words. Notice the scripture doesn't say to instruct or teach, but to train. In other words, we are to hedge our children in with the Word of God. We are to give them a complete series of instructions for every step they are to take in their lives.

---

[41] *Proverbs 22:6* - *[6]Train up a child in the way he should go: and when he is old, he will not depart from it. (KJV)*

We are to be like the drill sergeant and thoroughly train them in their duties. We are to teach them how to escape danger and how to appropriate the blessings of God. We need to impact their lives so much in the ways of God that it will become like a reflex to their nature. As parents, we also need to blanket them in prayer and instill in them the fear of God. But how can we do this as parents if we don't see how vital it is?

The word *train* here is also compared to a boxer and his trainer. The trainer of an athlete doesn't just tell the athlete to go train and then just sit around and watch television, hoping the athlete follows their instructions. No, they are right there with them every step of the way. A trainer doesn't tell their athlete to get up at 4am in the morning then sleep in till noon. He's up at 4am with them, pushing them, encouraging them and running alongside them.

It upsets me sometimes when I see how diligent parents are with their children when it comes to sports, education and secular activities and yet are lackadaisical when it comes to the things of God.

The Seriousness of Raising God-Fearing Children

Deuteronomy 21:18-21 says, *"If a man have a stubborn and rebellious son, which will not obey the voice of his father, or the voice of his mother, and that, when they have chastened him, will not hearken unto them: Then shall his father and his mother lay hold on him, and bring him out unto the elders of his city, and unto the gate of his place; And they shall say unto the elders of his city, This our son is stubborn and rebellious, he will not obey our voice; he is a glutton, and a drunkard. And all the men of his city shall stone him with stones, that he die: so shalt thou put evil away from among you; and all Israel shall hear, and fear."* (KJV)

Now this is serious, isn't it? Thank God we are no longer under the old covenant traditions and ceremonies. However, the seriousness of raising children in today's society is imperative for us to grasp. This child was being chastened by his parents, but he didn't heed to their chastening. So, the parents then presented him to the elders and explained their situation.

Look at what the elders did. The men of the city stoned the disobedient son to death. This is an absolute horrible picture of dealing with an unruly child. But, as we read on we see the significance was a serious issue. This was an evil that was dealt with very harshly. Don't get me wrong. I'm not for this type of punishment nor am I implying it needs to be done today. The point I want to draw attention to is that a rebellious child needs to be dealt with in respect to the evil they can spread.

Look at the world today. Grade school children are taking guns to class and killing innocent students, teenagers die just about every day from a drive-by shooting, and incidents of rape, molestation, bullying and violence are running rampant in our young people. This is the result of God being shut out of the world. It is the result of the spirit of anti-Christ being allowed to invade our families and marriages. And, yes, it is even rampant in Christian homes today.

The Old Testament tradition we find in Deuteronomy 21: 18-21 is horrific to say the least, but the result of not training our children in the ways of God is maybe even more horrific. Your child, that little innocent baby, has the potential of helping a troubled world or adding to its denigration. So, let's take Proverbs 22:6 a little more serious and heed to the word of God when it comes to raising our children.

Duties of Parents

Proverbs 23:13-14 says, *"Withhold not correction from the child: for if thou beatest him with the rod, he shall not die. Thou shalt beat him with the rod, and shalt deliver his soul from hell."* (KJV)

Let's look at a few words here. The word **rod** in the Hebrew means a stick or branch used for punishing. We will look more closely at the word punishment later. According to this scripture we are not to withhold correction, not punishment. Our mindset needs to change in this area. Correction is not punishment. Correction brings life and salvation, which is if we believe the Word of God. We need to see how serious of an issue this really is. Our duty as a parent is to correct, not punish.

In Proverbs 13:24 the Scripture says, *"He that spareth his rod hateth his son: but he that loveth him chasteneth him betimes."* (KJV) He that spares the rod hates his son... are we getting this? This is not at all popular with today's parents. But, true love corrects, because true love has the child's spiritual destiny in mind. It goes on to say... 'but he who loves him chastens him.'

Proverbs 19:18 – *"Chasten thy son while there is hope, and let not thy soul spare for his crying."* (KJV) Remember we learned that a child extends from infancy to adolescence, but here is where it gets a little bit touchy. We may correct a child until they start playing on our emotions. Then, when they start crying or pleading with us to stop, we often times do. Not only do we stop correcting them, we tend to pick them up and start pampering them. When we do this, we just negated any and all correction. The child now thinks we are apologizing for correcting them; that we are in the wrong. The child will also connect this reaction to stopping the correction to be used again.

Proverbs 22:15 – *"Foolishness is bound in the heart of a child; but the rod of correction shall drive it far from him."* (KJV) This is why correction is a must. Doing the opposite of how they are instructed or to rebel comes naturally to a child. The word **bound** in the Hebrew means to tie; to physically gird or confine. It also means conspiracy or to conspire against. The word *foolishness* in the Hebrew means evil; silliness and perverseness. It's natural for a child to conspire against their parents. But, the rod of correction shall drive it far from them. Scripture doesn't say that instruction will drive it away, but the rod of correction. It also doesn't say time out or grounding; it says the 'rod'.

Here are some keys to discipline. The Bible says if we spare the rod, it doesn't say we have to use it every time. The rod, along with instruction or verbal commands, will bring obedience. The rod is to be used if the child doesn't respond to your voice. The rod isn't to be the first means of correction, but to be used if necessary. Sparing or withholding the rod of correction does extremely more damage to a child than using it.

Most importantly, the rod is to be used in love, not out of anger or revenge.

Chapter 8

Finances

These last three chapters deal mostly with the parental duties, especially with each other. A strong relationship with God is the foundation for a strong family. A strong relationship between husbands and wives is the framework. The three areas I'm going to focus on in Christian marriages are Finances, Communication and Intimacy.

The Bible states in [42]Ecclesiastes 10:19 that money answers all things. The quest for financial freedom has always been at the top of people's hopes and dreams. Over the years of ministry, my wife and I have counseled many married couples and found finances to be a major problem area. Even to the place of the word 'divorce' coming up in these sessions. Also as with Pastors, the subject of money or giving can be a touchy subject.

---

[42] <u>Ecclesiastes 10:19</u> – *[19]A feast is made for laughter, and wine maketh merry: but money answereth all things. (KJV)*

If there is an area in which our homes and families need to have a God-given revelation, it is with money and giving. A house that serves God is a house that not only gives itself, but also its finances into God's hands.

I can remember when Carla and I first accepted Jesus as Lord. We had been married several years and had all our debts well established. I'm sure everyone can relate. We started attending the church where we were saved on a regular basis. We soon found ourselves at a crisis of faith and in a dilemma. We didn't have any money left over to tithe. We had all of our hard-earned money accounted for before we even got our paycheck. So, to make a long story short... we didn't tithe. Then one day when I was at work the Spirit of the Lord started dealing with me on the subject. He asked me how I could trust Him for the biggest things in my life, but not trust Him with my money. To my surprise, my wife was having the same experience at home. Upon my arrival from work, I found my wife waiting for me in our living room. When our eyes met, I knew what she was going to say. "Honey, we need to start tithing!" We started the next Sunday and haven't stopped since.

Giving is the very nature of God and a house that serves God is a giving house. Not just dad and mom, but everyone.

God's Plan for Financial Prosperity

In [43]Luke 6:38 scripture says, *"Give and it shall be given."* But, it doesn't stop there. Look how it shall be given: *"Good measure, pressed down, shaken together and running over. Men shall give to us who give to God!"* But, watch this… *"for with the same measure we mete (or measure), it shall be measured to us again."* Wow, we control what comes into our households by what goes out of our households!

We see this same principle again in 2 Corinthians 9:6 – *"But this I say, He which soweth sparingly shall reap also sparingly; and he which soweth bountifully shall reap also bountifully."* What

---

[43] *Luke 6:38* – [38]*Give, and it shall be given unto you; good measure, pressed down, and shaken together, and running over, shall men give into your bosom. For with the same measure that ye mete withal it shall be measured to you again. (KJV)*

we give and how much we give determines what and how much we get. The simplicity of financial prosperity is giving, and giving with the right attitude. We complicate this by holding back or justifying not giving at all.

Dangers of Keeping for Ourselves

Here is a story of a household, a husband and wife, who kept for themselves. We find that back in Acts chapter 4 many people were selling their lands and houses and giving the money to the Apostles to be used in the ministry. Wow, think about that. The early church must have been very prosperous. This giving was a voluntary act, but there was a specific couple, Ananias and Sapphira, in [44]Chapter 5 who decided to

---

[44] *Acts 5:1-10* – *But a certain man named Ananias, with Sapphira his wife, sold a possession, And kept back part of the price, his wife also being privy to it, and brought a certain part, and laid it at the apostles' feet.But Peter said, Ananias, why hath Satan filled thine heart to lie to the Holy Ghost, and to keep back part of the price of the land? Whiles it remained, was it not thine own? and after it was sold, was it not in thine own power? why hast thou conceived this thing in thine heart? thou hast not lied unto men, but unto God. And Ananias hearing these words fell down, and gave up the ghost: and great fear came on all them that heard these things.And the young men arose, wound him up, and carried him out, and buried him. And it was about the space of three hours after, when his wife, not knowing what was done, came in. And Peter answered unto her, Tell me whether ye sold the land for so much? And she said, Yea, for so much. Then Peter said unto her, How is it that ye have agreed together to tempt the Spirit of the Lord? behold, the feet of them which have buried thy husband are at the door, and shall carry thee out. Then*

keep a portion of their proceeds for themselves. They agreed together to this deception and chose to tempt the Spirit of God. Look at how powerful or deadly it is (depending on how you want to look at it) for a household to hold back from God. Scripture says that great fear came upon all the church and upon everyone who heard the story. You see, as parents, we must lead by example and show our children to give through our own giving.

True Financial Prosperity

Now, let's look at God's plan for success. In [45]Joshua 1:8 the scriptures states that the Word must be taught and adhered to in our homes, and after we have meditated on God's Word day and night and observed to do all that is written in it, THEN our way will be prosperous and we shall have good success. The word *way* in the Hebrew means the road that is trodden or

---

fell she down straightway at his feet, and yielded up the ghost: and the young men came in, and found her dead, and, carrying her forth, buried her by her husband. (KJV)

[45] *Joshua 1:8* – *[8]This book of the law shall not depart out of thy mouth; but thou shalt meditate therein day and night, that thou mayest observe to do according to all that is written therein: for then thou shalt make thy way prosperous, and then thou shalt have good success. (KJV)*

course of life. Are we getting this? If we want good success through the course of our lives, we are to be a house that is sold out to God. The word *prosperous* in the Hebrew means profitable. This is God's plan for success.

Notice the words 'good success'. Does this mean there could be bad success? Let's think about this for a minute. It's been my observation that success can change people. The bible clearly states in [46]Matthew 19:23 that rich men can hardly enter into the Kingdom of God. In [47]Luke 12:20 we heard the story of a rich man who had lots of stuff, but didn't have Jesus. God called this man a fool. Now the point here is not that people who have a lot of money aren't going to heaven, but that not all success is profitable or good for us. Being successful and the love of money can be a stumbling block when it comes to loving and serving

---

[46] *Matthew 19:23* – *[23]Then said Jesus unto his disciples, Verily I say unto you, That a rich man shall hardly enter into the kingdom of heaven. (KJV)*

[47] *Luke 12:20* – *[20]But God said unto him, Thou fool, this night thy soul shall be required of thee: then whose shall those things be, which thou hast provided? (KJV)*

God. That is why it is so important for our families and homes to serve the Lord.

Allow me to end this section with a challenge to you and your family. Parents, I can't express how vital it is it teach and train your family in Biblical giving. A house that gives will be a blessed house. It's important to see that your children get a good education and be successful in life, however never allow the success that the world has to offer become more important than the success of a Godly home.

My wife Carla and I are blessed beyond measure. It's not because of anything material we have, although we are very grateful to God for it, it's because of the family that God has blessed us with. There is no amount of money or worldly treasure that can compare to a family that loves and serves the Lord. A blessed house is a house that has turned its finances over to God.

Chapter 9

Communication

A healthy marriage and family depends on communication. In this day and age in which we live, communication is essential. We are exposed to all kinds of activities that demand our time and attention. We have cell phones, regular phones, texting, social networks and answering services and that just names a few, yet I still have a hard time reaching people sometimes.

The intimate contact with one another is becoming a thing of the past. I asked one of our teenagers in our youth group about texting. She told me that she like to text because if you decided to end the conversation all you had to do was stop texting. Although we stay in touch with people, the intimate contact of fellowship is in danger. This can become critical, especially to a marriage or family.

I can remember when eating together as a family was a priority even to the place if I had missed supper because I was outside playing, I missed supper. Dinnertime was a time of communicating with one another as a family.

In the armed forces communication is vital. Battles and wars have been lost simply because of a lack of communication. As a matter of fact, our enemies try to destroy communication because they know how vitally important it is when they plan to attack. On this note, don't you think that our enemy wants to break communication between husbands and wives, parents and children, and most of all us and God? Sure he does. In counseling, one of the major target areas is communication. With statements made quite often to the effect of, "I didn't know he felt that way" or "I didn't know she thought that way."

Communication in Marriage

In [48]I Peter 3:7 the Word states that husbands are to give honor to their wives. One of the greatest ways to show respect and honor is to communicate with each other. As I have stated previously, a man's rule over his wife is not one of dominance, but one of respect and honor. The word *honor* here means to deem very valuable. If we deem our wives as valuable, then we must value their aspirations and input into our marriages and families.

I have found with our two boys that my wife could communicate with them in ways I could not, and vice versa. To not listen to her advice and opinion about matters in their lives would not only be unwise but disrespectful. I might add… that goes the other way also.

A lack of communication will result in either the husband or the wife making a family decision on their own, or making a decision that one or the other didn't

---

[48] *1 Peter 3:7* – *⁷Likewise, ye husbands, dwell with them according to knowledge, giving honour unto the wife, as unto the weaker vessel, and as being heirs together of the grace of life; that your prayers be not hindered. (KJV)*

know anything about. Needless to say, this is fuel for a time of intense fellowship.

Marriages and families need to make it a priority to communicate with one another. My wife and I talk a lot and share our feelings with one another. I have to say, I don't agree with her feelings all the time, and she doesn't always agree with mine. But, I do try to understand her thoughts and feelings based on the person I've come to know and love. I can remember when we were dating and spent hours on the phone, hating to get off. We were like that commercial on television where we counted to three so both of us could hang up at the same time only to realize neither one of us wanted to. Marriages need to rekindle that kind of relationship. Communication is a very important factor in a marriage and we need to keep it strong and active.

Communication between Parents and Children

It states in [49]Ephesians 6:4 not to provoke our children, to do or say things that we know will cause them pain or make them angry. This doesn't mean we are not to give them advice that might make them angry, but we're not to be abusive in the kind of correction we give them. Godly correction will sometimes make them angry. For example, after you and your spouse have prayed and come to a decision that they can't spend the night or go to the concert, or have to miss the party because it's in their best interest, they won't like those decisions and it won't sit well with them. Most likely they'll play the, "you just don't trust me" card. But, hang in there because you can never go wrong by doing what you know to be right.

I can remember when decisions my wife and I made with our boys that weren't popular. They weren't happy about them. However, if you ask them today they would admit they were the right decisions. As a matter

---

[49] _Ephesians 6:4_ – ⁴*And, ye fathers, provoke not your children to wrath: but bring them up in the nurture and admonition of the Lord. (KJV)*

of fact, I now see them and their wives making many of those same decisions with their children.

Making Godly decisions for and about our children is one of the greatest acts of pure love. They may not think so at the time, but when they get older they will be glad you did. Our communication to our children needs to be Godly and respectful. The way we communicate to them is most likely how they will communicate with others.

How we communicate with and to others make a difference. Let it always be with grace and seasoned with salt. This means let it be holy, wise, gracious, respectful, courteous and worthy of remembrance. If we are instructed to do this to everyone, how much more important is it to do in our marriage and families?

Chapter 10

Intimacy

The definition of intimacy is closely acquainted or associated with being private or personal. Intimacy is another problem area in families and especially marriages. It is shown in different ways. Simply being interested in your spouse's days to the point of wanting to know how their day went can be very intimate.

God desires a husband and wife to experience intimacy with each other. In ongoing healthy relationships between husbands and wives, intimacy is essential to their family. My sons have commented several times about how they saw their mother and me giving each other little smooches and hugs as they were growing up. Still to this day, they give their mother and me pecks on the cheek with a "I love you Mom and Dad" every time they see us. This is precious to me because now their children see it and follow in their footsteps.

God has a lot to say about intimacy in His Word. It's the world's abuse and misguidance that has turned intimacy into a perversion or taboo.

God's Advice on Intimacy

1 Corinthians 7:3-5 states: *³"Let the husband render unto the wife due benevolence: and likewise also the wife unto the husband. ⁴The wife hath not power of her own body, but the husband: and likewise also the husband hath not power of his own body, but the wife. ⁵Defraud ye not one the other, except it be with consent for a time, that ye may give yourselves to fasting and prayer; and come together again, that Satan tempt you not for your incontinency."* I want to remind you that this is New Testament teaching. The Apostle Paul was very explicit and to the point here and according to verse 1 was important enough that the Corinthian church wrote to Paul concerning this matter. The physical and sexual aspects of marriage are not something that should be shoved under the rug in a Christian home. They need to be talked about and understood. We must remember that if God hadn't sanctioned sex, it wouldn't exist.

However, God intended it to occur only in marriage and only between the husband and wife.

In verse 3, the word **benevolence** here means good will and kindness. It means to have and show mutual respect for each other. In this particular chapter it's in reference to sexual relationships.

In verse 4, this shows how husbands and wives belong to one another. This is just another example of God's equality between man and woman. Neither is superior or inferior to the other. This is opposite of what worldly philosophy teaches.

The Danger of Unbalanced and Misused Relationships

In [50]1 Corinthians 7:5 we notice that the scripture states '*husbands and wives*', not men and women. My point is this; Paul here refers to a married couple. The word **defraud** here in the original language means to

---

[50] *1 Corinthians 7:5* - [5]*Defraud ye not one the other, except it be with consent for a time, that ye may give yourselves to fasting and prayer; and come together again, that Satan tempt you not for your incontinency. (KJV)*

deprive or keep back by fraud. Now, I don't know how deep we want to investigate this, but it goes pretty deep.

My wife and I have counseled couples that have held back on one another, either because of an argument or to use it to manipulate one another. This is wrong. According to God's Word we are not to do this. It should go without saying that if a husband or wife has problems or a problem with intimacy, they should seek wise counsel. Allow me to interject something here. Men should never counsel women alone, or women should not counsel men alone. But, let's move on. The only reason a husband or wife should deprive one another of sexual intimacy is because of fasting or prayer, and then only if it is agreed upon by both spouses. A lack of sexual intimacy can give the enemy a foothold in a marriage. Sadly to say, my wife and I have witnessed this more times than we'd like to share, where either the husband or wife had a problem physically, emotionally or spiritually and they didn't seek help in any of those areas only to find themselves in a marriage deep in trouble.

In the Song of Solomon, God thought intimacy was so important that He devoted an entire book to it. You need to read and study the Song of Solomon and ask God's wisdom concerning intimacy.

Hebrews 13:4 says – *"Marriage is honorable in all, and the bed undefiled: but whoremongers and adulterers God will judge."* This is a principle for Christian marriages. The word **honorable** means to be held in the highest regard and to be cherished above all other relationships. When the Bible says the bed is undefiled, this means unstained by sin and any defilement. God encourages husbands and wives to engage in sexual intimacy. As you read the Song of Solomon, you will find and see the passion that God desires for a husband and wife to have toward one another. God made a husband and wife to be fully satisfied with one another, but only with one another. Today, sexual freedom is a perversion of what God intended for the marriage. But, it should be of no surprise to the Christian household. The enemy wants and tries to discredit and destroy everything God intended to be good, holy and pure.

I hope you have enjoyed this book and that your spiritual eyes have been opened to the important role that each family member is in relationship to each other, and most importantly in relation to God. I pray that you find revelation in these words and you apply these principles to your life and they become a blessing to you and your family.

Allow me to end this book with this: Husbands and fathers, declare and decree before men and God; "As for me and my house, we will serve the Lord!"

~Rev. Daniel L. Patrick

About the Author

Reverend Daniel L. Patrick and his wife Carla have served as Senior Pastors at Deeper Life Christian Center in Carrollton, Georgia for over 20 years. They currently live in Bowdon, Georgia and have two sons Joey & Todd, daughter-in-laws Mechelle and Deanna, and four grandchildren Elise, Bailey, Garrett and Luke.

Deeper Life Christian Center
1860 N. Hwy 113
Carrollton, GA 30117
www.deeperlifechristiancenter.org (website)
deepercenter@deeperlifechristiancenter.org (email)

www.ingramcontent.com/pod-product-compliance
Lightning Source LLC
Chambersburg PA
CBHW060342050426
42449CB00011B/2813